Marcy Schaaf
Picky Eater Pete
AF441093

Once upon a time in a town not so far away, lived a little boy named Pete. Pete was known far and wide as the pickiest eater in the land. While other kids savored all sorts of delicious dishes, Pete had a list of only five foods he would even consider: pizza, hotdogs, chicken nuggets, bananas, and mac and cheese. To Pete, everything else looked strange and, frankly, a little bit silly.

But little did Pete know, an adventure was about to begin—one that would take him on a culinary journey full of wiggly noodles, fishy sticks, green goo, and many other surprising delights. Join Pete as he discovers that trying new foods can be a whole lot of fun, and sometimes, even the silliest looking food can turn out to be delicious!

Pete was the pickiest eater in town.

He only liked five foods: pizza, hotdogs, chicken nuggets, bananas, and mac and cheese.

Pete's mom made spaghetti for dinner.

"Ew!" said Pete. "It looks like worms!"

"Try it,"
said Mom.
"Worms are yummy!"

Pete took a tiny bite. "Wiggly, but tasty!"

The next day, Grandpa made fish sticks.

"Fishy sticks? No thanks!" Pete laughed.

"Just one bite," Grandpa encouraged.

Pete tried one. "Swimmy, but delicious!"

At school Pete's friend Sam had sushi.

"Raw fish? Gross!" Pete giggled.

"Just a taste,"
said Sam.
"You'll like it."

Pete tried. "Slimy, but yummy!"

At Grandma's, Pete saw broccoli soup.

"Green goo? No way!" Pete shrieked.

"Give it a try,"
said Grandma.
"You'll see."

Pete took a sip. "Silly, but tasty!"

Pete's sister made a blueberry pie.

"Sticky goo? Ew!" Pete said.

"Just one bite,"
his sister said.

Pete nibbled. "Sticky, but good!"

One day, Pete saw a new fruit.

"What's this?" he asked.

“It’s a mango,”
Mom said.
“Try it.”

Pete took a bite. "Weird, but delicious!"

Pete realized trying new foods was fun.

He discovered many new favorites.

Pete was no longer a picky eater.

Now, mealtime was a fun adventure!

The End.

Pete learned to try funny foods.

What new foods have you tried?

Books By Schaaf

www.BookBySchaaf.com

Find us at: